SPORTS GREAT
MAGIC
JOHNSON

Revised and Expanded

—*Sports Great Books*—

Sports Great Charles Barkley (ISBN 0-89490-386-1)

Sports Great Larry Bird (ISBN 0-89490-368-3)

Sports Great Roger Clemens (ISBN 0-89490-284-9)

Sports Great John Elway (ISBN 0-89490-282-2)

Sports Great Patrick Ewing (ISBN 0-89490-369-1)

Sports Great Bo Jackson (ISBN 0-89490-281-4)

Sports Great Magic Johnson (Revised and Expanded)
(ISBN 0-89490-160-5)

Sports Great Michael Jordan (ISBN 0-89490-370-5)

Sports Great Joe Montana (ISBN 0-89490-371-3)

Sports Great Hakeem Olajuwon (ISBN 0-89490-372-1)

Sports Great David Robinson (ISBN 0-89490-373-X)

Sports Great Darryl Strawberry (ISBN 0-89490-291-1)

Sports Great Isiah Thomas (ISBN 0-89490-374-8)

Sports Great Herschel Walker (ISBN 0-89490-207-5)

SPORTS GREAT MAGIC JOHNSON

Revised and Expanded

James Haskins

—Sports Great Books—

ENSLOW PUBLISHERS, INC.

Bloy St. & Ramsey Ave. P.O. Box 38
Box 777 Aldershot
Hillside, N.J. 07205 Hants GU12 6BP
U.S.A. U.K.

Library of Congress Cataloging-in-Publication Data

Haskins, James, 1941-
    Sports great Magic Johnson / James Haskins. — Rev. and expanded.
      p. cm. —
    Includes index.
    Summary: A biography of the superstar basketball player, from his
childhood through his career with the Los Angeles Lakers to his
present HIV-positive status and campaign against AIDS.
    ISBN 0-89490-348-9
    1. Johnson, Earvin, 1959-   —Juvenile literature. 2. Basketball
players—United States—Biography—Juvenile literature. 3. AIDS
(Disease)—Patients—United States—Biography—Juvenile literature.
[1. Johnson, Earvin, 1959-   . 2. Basketball players. 3. Afro
-Americans—Biography.] I. Title.

GV884. J63H38 1992
796.323'092—dc20
[B]
                                  92-9188
                                       CIP
                                       AC

Printed in the United State of America

10 9 8 7 6 5 4 3 2 1

Illustration Credits:
Brian Burd, Lansing State Journal, p. 12; George Fox, p. 15; Los Angeles Lakers, p. 45;
Michigan State University, pp. 21, 25, 27; United Press International, p. 36; AP/Wide World
Photos, pp. 8, 31, 42, 49, 52, 54, 57, 59, 61, 65, 71, 73, 76.

Contents

Chapter 1 7

Chapter 2 19

Chapter 3 29

Chapter 4 38

Chapter 5 47

Chapter 6 56

Chapter 7 63

Career Statistics 78

Index 79

Acknowledgments

I am grateful to George Fox for his time and his help in providing information and photographs. Thanks are due also to the Los Angeles Lakers organization, to Fred Stabley, Jr., and Fred Stabley, Sr., and to Nick Vista, Director of Sports Information at Michigan State University. A special thank-you to Ann Jefferies for her research help, and to Kathy Benson for her work in helping to pull everything together.

Chapter 1

In May 1987, Earvin "Magic" Johnson was named the Most Valuable Player of the National Basketball Association. It was the first time in his eight-year career in pro basketball that he had received this honor. It was also the first time in over 20 years that a guard had been named the MVP.

Usually, forwards and centers get the award. They are the ones who score the most points and pull down the most rebounds. But once in a while a guard comes along who can score points and get rebounds and also make so many great passes that he is obviously one of the main reasons for his team's success. Such a situation had occurred exactly twice before in NBA history. In 1957, Bob Cousy of the Boston Celtics won the MVP award. In 1964 that honor went to Oscar Robertson of Cincinnati. And now, 23 years later, the prize was Magic Johnson's.

On the basketball court, Magic Johnson is a team player. He is just as happy making a great pass so that a teammate can score as he is making a basket himself. As a matter of fact, he sometimes will pass off to a teammate when he has a clear shot himself. People also marvel at his "court sense." He always seems to know where everyone else is as both teams run up and down the court. Magic developed his unselfishness and his court sense during his many years of playing basketball. But he was a "team player" practically from the time he was born. He was one of eight children. Add two parents, and you have a family of ten, large enough for two basketball teams!

Magic grins as he accepts the MVP award for 1986-1987. It's the first time he has won, and only the third time in NBA history that a guard has been given the award.

Magic was born on August 14, 1959, the sixth child of Earvin and Christine Johnson. He was the second boy, but he, not his older brother Larry, was the one who was named Earvin Johnson, Jr. It was not until many years later that he got the nickname "Magic."

Earvin's father worked in the Oldsmobile auto plant in Lansing, Michigan, where they lived. He also held two part-time jobs in order to support such a big family. Earvin's mother worked just as hard raising all those children.

Earvin and the other Johnson boys started playing basketball as soon as they could handle the ball. Both their parents had been basketball players when they were younger. During the basketball season each year, Mr. Johnson would watch the games on television whenever he had the chance. While his children watched with him, he explained how the game was played.

Earvin loved basketball so much that even in the middle of winter he would shovel the snow off the court at the Main Street School playground so he could practice. He was always on the court by 7:30 A.M. The neighbors on Middle Street, seeing him hopping around the court as they set off for work, took to calling him "June Bug Johnson." "There's that crazy June Bug, hoppin'," they'd say.

When he was in the fourth grade, Earvin met a boy his own age on the playground of the Main Street School. The boy's name was Jay Vincent, and he loved basketball as much as Earvin did. The two started playing together often, and before long they were best friends. There were usually many other boys who wanted to play in the school yard, and the only way you could keep playing was to keep winning. That's why Earvin relied on what he calls his "hoopsy doopsy style." He drove for lay-ups and the sure two points instead of taking risks with outside shots.

By the time he entered Dwight Rich Junior High School, Earvin had grown to be six feet tall. He was very skinny and lacked power, but he had remarkable coordination. He was not a high scorer, but he was an excellent passer. He seemed to have a better sense of what was happening on the court than most boys his age. What's more, he played basketball with a total joy that made the game more fun for his teammates.

When he was still in junior high school, people began to notice how good Earvin was at basketball. Many high school coaches became interested in him. One was George Fox, the coach at Everett High School in Lansing. He remembers, "We were all aware in junior high school that he'd be all-state some day."

George Fox did not think he would ever get a chance to coach Earvin Johnson. In those days, the students at Everett High School, which was located in a white section of Lansing, were almost all white. Earvin Johnson lived closest to Sexton High School, which was almost all black. Both George Fox and Earvin Johnson thought that Earvin would go to Sexton.

Then, when Earvin was in the ninth grade, the Lansing school board voted to bring racial integration to the schools by busing students to schools outside their neighborhoods. Earvin learned that he would be attending Everett High, and he did not like it. "I was upset," he said later. "I wanted to go to Sexton. I went to every Sexton game. I was a Sexton man, and then they came up with this busing thing."

The first year at Everett High was hard for Earvin.

Although the busing program brought a number of blacks to the school, they were still a small part of the total school population. Earvin had grown up in a black neighborhood and had gone to black schools. Attending a mostly white school was a new experience.

Earvin was also going through the same difficulties that most teenagers have. He was no longer a child, but he wasn't yet an adult. His parents were very strict, and he felt they treated him as a child. He resented that. He was at times moody and sulky.

The one thing that made high school bearable for Earvin that first year was basketball. He made friends with members of the team. The first was Reggie Chastine, one year ahead of him, who had also come to Everett as a result of the busing program. The 5-foot-6-inch guard enjoyed ball-handling, making lots of assists, and having fun playing the game, just as Earvin did. Once the basketball season began, Earvin made a lot of other friends.

He was the team's high scorer and top rebounder in almost every game. He also made the greatest number of assists. He was a hero to his fellow students, and before long his sulky, moody manner disappeared. In its place was a smile as wide as his Afro hairstyle.

Soon, he was also a celebrity outside the school. Everyone who followed high-school basketball knew about him. His name made headlines in the local newspapers. Sportswriters could not say enough good things about him. One sports reporter, Fred Stabley, Jr., of *The Lansing State Journal,* wrote in early December 1974 that Earvin Johnson was magic on the court. That's how 15-year-old Earvin got the nickname, "Magic."

In spite of great won-lost records during the regular

11

Earvin Johnson towers over his friend Reggie Chastine as they discuss strategy at an Everett High School game.

season, the Everett High Vikings could not seem to keep winning during the state championship series. In Earvin's second year on the team, the Vikings were knocked out in the quarterfinals. Earvin sat down and cried. He finished out the year as the team's leading scorer, leading rebounder, and leader in assists, but he would have preferred to be a member of the state championship team.

By the time Earvin started his junior year at Everett, he had learned better how to accept losing. After 11 games and a record of 11–0, the Vikings lost to Detroit Northeastern by five points. Earvin took the loss hard, but by this time, as George Fox puts it, he was "a quick recoverer."

There were very few losses to be accepted that season. In fact, the Vikings had more blowouts than ever that year. In one game against Sexton, Earvin actually scored 54 points, setting a city-wide high-school scoring record. (Later, Earvin's sister Evelyn broke that record in her senior year.)

The next game, Earvin's shooting was off, so he concentrated on making assists. When the game was over, he had *16* of them. Asked which he had enjoyed more, the points or the assists, he did not have to think about his answer. "The assists," he said with a grin. "I like to pass, hit the open man. I like to see somebody else enjoying it."

The Vikings reached the semifinals in the state tournament that season. But Detroit Catholic Central knocked them out of the tournament with a 68–60 win. Earvin had 30 points and nine rebounds, but he fouled out with 1:29 left on the clock. Catholic Central made seven of its last nine points on free throws.

Although by now he had learned not to cry, Earvin blamed himself for the loss. What bothered him most was his feeling that he had let his friend, Reggie Chastine, down. It was Reggie's last year at Everett. Since he wasn't going to college and was too short to play pro basketball, that game against Detroit Catholic Central was his last chance at a championship. Reggie was named to the All-Capital Area Conference and All Metro-All Conference first teams, but Earvin knew he would rather have been a member of the state championship team.

Earvin was named to those first teams along with Reggie. He was also chosen for the Associated Press and United Press International "All State" teams and was named All Conference Most Valuable Player and United Press International's "Prep Player of the Year" in Michigan. He was his team's leading scorer, leading rebounder, and leader in assists and steals.

That summer Reggie Chastine was killed in an automobile accident. Earvin was deeply affected by the death of his closest friend. He realized the same thing could have happened to anyone, even to him, and he appreciated more than ever the gift of being alive.

Despite the tragedy of Reggie's death, life was beginning to get exciting for Earvin Johnson. He was among the top five high-school basketball players in the country. Already he was getting letters from five or six colleges every day. Earvin thought he would like to get a degree in communications and become a television reporter. But mostly he wanted to play college basketball. Basketball was his first love. It was a beautiful game, an exciting game, and a game at which he could win.

But first he had his senior year of basketball to enjoy.

In high school, Earvin was so good that by his junior year he was one of the top five high-school players in the country.

When the season began, Earvin dedicated it to Reggie, and his teammates did the same. But Earvin started out the season as if he were playing for both himself and Reggie. He was averaging over 40 points a game. Coach Fox finally reminded him that he did have four teammates, and Earvin concentrated more on assists.

The Vikings were Number 1 in the state during most of the season and were determined to go all the way that year. In the state tournament they won the regional finals, the quarterfinals, and the semifinals. They faced Birmingham's Brother Rice High in the championship game. It was one of the toughest games the Vikings had ever played.

In overtime, Everett fans started chanting, "Earvin Johnson! Earvin Johnson!" They kept it up as the clock wound down and the Vikings won by six points. The final score was 62–56. As people screamed and jumped around him, Earvin grew quiet for a time, thinking of Reggie.

Earvin was again named all-this and best-that. This time, however, UPI named him "Prep Player of the Year" not just for Michigan but for the whole country. But by now, Earvin was concentrating on the choice of a college.

Earvin had decided to attend either Michigan State University over in East Lansing or the University of Michigan at Ann Arbor. Before he made his final decision, he spent his spring vacation in Europe at the Albert Schweitzer games in Germany. When he stepped from the plane that brought him home, a huge crowd was waiting to welcome him. Half of them were waving University of Michigan banners. The other half had MSU banners.

It was a tough decision for Earvin to make. He liked the coaches at both schools. The University of Michigan had a better basketball program, and the idea of going to a school with a winning team appealed to him. MSU's program had practically fallen apart a couple of years back, due to a scandal over special favors to athletes. Since then, the new coach, Jud Heathcote, had been trying to rebuild the program. But that kind of rebuilding took time.

Earvin's father wanted him to go to Michigan State. Earvin thought about it for a while and decided he liked the prospect of playing on an underdog team and helping it to change from a loser to a winner. Besides, his playground basketball friend, Jay Vincent, was going to MSU. At the end of April 1977, Earvin made his decision to go to MSU. He then decided to enjoy his last weeks of high school.

In May, he turned down an invitation to play in the annual Michigan Roundball Classic in Detroit. It was scheduled for the same time as his senior prom pictures. There would be many more basketball classics, but there would only be one high school senior prom.

Chapter 2

Earvin didn't want to miss out on any part of college life by living at home and driving to MSU every day. He moved into one of the dormitories on campus. That way he could be on his own, but he could still go home whenever he wanted to.

Basketball practice would not start for a couple of months, so Earvin decided to study as hard as he could in the meantime. But he also had fun going to parties and dating the new girls he met. He was the best-known freshman on campus, and everyone at MSU hoped he would turn the basketball team into a winner. The Spartans had not won a conference title in 20 years. Both Earvin, as point guard, and Jay Vincent, as center, were expected to help junior Gregory Kelser, who was the team's high scorer.

Earvin enjoyed playing with his new teammates and became good friends off the court with Greg Kelser. With Kelser, Jay Vincent, and his other teammates, he put together a real team effort. By the end of February, with a win over Northwestern, the Spartans had won 20 games—more than any MSU team had won in a season in 79 years! Earvin finished the regular season first in the conference in assists, tied for third in scoring, fifth in free-throw percentage, and tied for sixth in rebounding. He was the only freshman named to an All-American team. And he was the only freshman selected to play for the U.S. college team that would play Cuba, Yugoslavia, and the Soviet Union that spring.

But the NCAA tournament was first. The National Collegiate Athletic Association tournament matches against one another the best college teams from around the nation. Though the Spartans made the tournament, they did not play in top form. They were knocked out by Western Kentucky in the tournament semifinals.

Earvin blamed himself for the loss, and that bothered some of his teammates. It seemed to them that if you were going to "talk team" in win situations, you ought to do the same when you lost. Now that they had lost, however, some members of the team let their resentment come out about all the glory Earvin usually received. They didn't put him down, but they did vote Greg Kelser the team's most valuable player. Earvin could not help being bothered by that.

By this time, many pro teams were urging him to leave college and turn pro. Under the rules of pro basketball, a college player can claim "hardship" and join a pro team before finishing college. Claiming hardship means that a player's family cannot really afford to keep him in college and needs the money that he will earn as a pro. Earvin wanted to turn pro. "It wasn't so much the fact of all that money as it was finally realizing the dream of being a professional that I've had so long," he said later.

In college, Magic discovered that he enjoyed being a ball handler as much as he enjoyed being a scorer.

Earvin's mother was against his leaving college. She wanted him to get his degree. His father was not so concerned about that, but he did not want Earvin to turn pro before he was ready. Earvin Johnson, Sr., finally decided that his son would be better off staying at MSU. Earvin went along with his father, but he later admitted that it was a hard decision to make. He had been offered as much as a quarter of a million dollars a season for six seasons. "They were talking a lot of money," said Earvin.

The Spartans started out well in the 1978–1979 season, but in January they lost four of their six games. Coach Heathcote realized that they were not playing as a team in the way they had the previous season. He decided to make some big changes. He moved Earvin from guard to forward, and after that the Spartans began to win again.

Earvin liked the change. It gave him more chances to bring the ball down the court and more freedom in moving the ball around under the basket. When the team started to win, he liked that, too. The Spartans ended their regular season with a record of 21–6 and another chance at the NCAA title. This time, they decided to treat every game in the tournament as if it were the championship game.

The Spartans first played Lamar College in Texas. Greg Kelser scored 31 points. Earvin Johnson had ten assists, most of them to Kelser. Jay Vincent sprained his ankle in the first half, but the Spartans still went on to trounce Lamar 95–64.

Next, the Spartans met the Louisiana State University Tigers. The Tigers' pre-game plan was to take an early lead and then freeze the ball the rest of the game.

Magic and Greg Kelser made sure that didn't happen. Kelser intercepted two passes and converted them into driving dunks. Then Magic really caught fire. He scored 24 points and had 12 assists, many of them expert passes that set up more dunks for Kelser. The Spartans won the game 79–71. But Jay Vincent suffered another injury, this time to his foot, and there was no one on the bench who could really take his place.

Against Notre Dame, the Spartans played the same five men while Notre Dame's coach, Digger Phelps, made a lot of lineup changes. Midway in the second half, with Michigan ahead by three points, Earvin Johnson and Greg Kelser really began to connect in a play called the lob and dunk. Earvin would pass a lob to Kelser, and Greg would dunk the ball. In a sudden spurt Greg scored seven straight baskets, four of them on passes from Earvin, to extend the lead from three to nine. The Notre Dame players didn't know what hit them. The Irish never got closer than seven points after that. The dunker wound up with 34 points, the passer with 13 assists. The win over Notre Dame advanced the Spartans to the NCAA semifinals, where the four remaining teams would play two contests on the same day at the University of Utah. Top-ranked Indiana State would play second-ranked DePaul after the third-ranked Spartans played the fourth-ranked Quakers of the University of Pennsylvania. The winners of the two contests would play each other for the championship.

In the first game, the Spartans were so much better than the Quakers that the game was no match. Earvin wound up with 29 points, 10 rebounds, and 10 assists. The Spartans team as a whole matched NCAA semifinals records in total points scored (101) and in the margin of winning points (34). But the fans became bored and started chanting "We want the Bird." They were calling for Larry Bird, star of the Indiana State team. If they had to watch a mismatched game, they at least wanted to watch one that Larry Bird was in.

Bird was a great scorer. He was even more famous than Magic Johnson because he had led his team to an amazing 32-game winning streak. Also, he was a senior and had been starring on the court for a longer time. Fans and reporters often compared Bird and Johnson, although their styles of play were very different. The comparisons had become "either-or" contests. You could not like them both; you had to like one or the other.

Johnson and Bird hardly knew each other. Their schools did not meet during the regular season. Neither player wanted to get caught up in the controversy, and both had only nice things to say about the other to reporters.

But what Earvin Johnson did not like was hearing the fans at the University of Utah Special Events Center calling for Larry Bird. After Indiana State beat DePaul in the next game, the stage was set for an exciting match between MSU and Indiana State. Earvin was determined to show the fans that he could outplay Bird.

But Coach Heathcote was not after a shoot-out between the two stars; he was after a win by his team. He set up a special zone defense against Bird, and Magic and the rest of the Spartans followed it. Bird's teammates had trouble getting the ball to him, and when he did get the ball, he had trouble getting off a shot. He shot only 7 for 21 and scored only 19 points. Meanwhile, Magic and the other Spartans put on a real show of teamwork with highly balanced scoring. Johnson led all

24

In the 1979 NCAA championship game against Indiana State University, Magic spent as much time making assists to his teammates as he did trying to score.

Spartans with 24 points; Kelser had 19; and guard Terry Donnelly, after averaging only 6.3 points in earlier tournament games, had 15 points. When the buzzer sounded, the Spartans had won 75–64.

MSU fans were screaming, "We're Number 1!" and under the basket Earvin Johnson and Greg Kelser hugged each other. Then Earvin looked over at Indiana State's bench and saw Larry Bird with his head buried in a towel. The grin of victory left Earvin's face. He knew how hard it was to lose. Later, Bird was named College Player of the Year. Magic would have liked to win that award, but he was happier to be a member of the NCAA championship team.

There was no letdown for Earvin. Once again he was faced with the choice of staying in college or turning pro. Everyone at MSU and every basketball fan in the state of Michigan wanted him to stay in college. His mother did, too. His father wanted to listen to what the pro teams had to offer. They had to decide soon. Magic would have to declare hardship status by May 11 in order to be eligible for the National Basketball Association draft on June 25.

Earvin wanted to turn pro. He promised his mother that he would go to summer school and earn his degree just as soon as he could. She seemed to be satisfied with that promise. Earvin's father felt that his son was now ready to play pro ball. All that was left were negotiations with the Los Angeles Lakers.

Several seasons before, the Lakers had obtained from the Utah Jazz the right to a first-round pick in the 1979 draft. If the Lakers won the coin toss that decided which team would pick first, the Lakers would be able to select whomever they wanted. They wanted Magic Johnson.

Magic and his teammates kept the ball away from Larry Bird in the 1979
NCAA championship game. Meanwhile, Magic scored 24 points.

Representatives from the Lakers met with Mr. and Mrs. Johnson and the agent that the family had hired to represent Earvin. They finally agreed on a contract that called for $600,000 a year for four years. Earvin knew that Larry Bird had signed with the Boston Celtics for $650,000 a year, but he was happy with the Lakers' offer. Six hundred thousand dollars a year was more than the Johnson family had ever expected to see.

The first thing Earvin wanted to do was to buy his family a new house and do something nice for each of his sisters and brothers. His parents and advisers told him not to spend the money before he even had it. They reminded him that making so much money was serious business. The money should be invested so that Earvin would have it in the future. At the age of 19, healthy and strong, Earvin felt as if he could play basketball forever. But there was always the possibility of injury. Even without injury, by the time he was in his early thirties, he would have to start thinking about retiring from the game. If he invested his basketball salary carefully, he would have something to show for his playing years besides trophies and yellowed newspaper clippings.

When the NBA draft opened on June 25, there wasn't much suspense about where Magic Johnson would play in his first pro season. Earlier, Los Angeles had won the coin toss against Chicago for the first pick in the draft. In the grand ballroom of the Plaza Hotel in New York City, the Lakers' representative spoke the name "Earvin Johnson" loudly and clearly. Moments later, Greg Kelser was drafted by the Detroit Pistons. Other names were spoken and other picks were made. After a while, the full reality of the moment dawned on Magic. "Wow," he said to himself, "on the same team as *Kareem Abdul-Jabbar!*"

Chapter 3

Professional basketball is a lot different from college basketball. First of all, it is a job. Even if you love playing basketball more than anything else in the world, it is still hard to play night after night during the long NBA season. Magic was used to a school basketball schedule of 20 to 30 games in five months. In the coming season with the Lakers, he would be playing at least 82 games in six months.

There would be long road trips, and that was something else Magic had not experienced before. A couple of away games a month in college basketball just does not prepare a player for the hardships of the NBA road schedule.

Another adjustment for Earvin was being a long way from home for the first time. Except for trips out of the country to play on U.S. basketball teams, Earvin had never really been out of Lansing, Michigan. Just finding an apartment of his own in Los Angeles was a new experience. His parents had warned him so often not to get caught up in the "Hollywood" style of life that he was almost afraid to go out.

But the major adjustments Magic had to make were to the rougher NBA game and to his new teammates.

Magic was not the only newcomer to the Lakers. The team had a new owner and a new coach. The change in leadership meant that the veteran players on the team would have to make some adjustments, too. During preseason training camp, Coach Jack McKinney decided that Earvin should be the chief ball-handling guard. Guard Norm Nixon had to give up his position to Magic.

Magic played his first regular-season game as a Laker on October 12, 1979, in San Diego against the Clippers. He made only one point in his first 17 minutes of play, and the coach took him out. Magic was not prepared for the roughness of the game. When Coach McKinney put him back in, he was ready. By the closing seconds, he had 26 points. It was a close game, but thanks to a hook shot by Abdul-Jabbar, the Lakers won it, 103–102.

In the weeks that followed, Magic showed that he could play the pro game. He didn't always score a lot, and he made plenty of mistakes, but he also made some spectacular plays. During the third quarter of a game against San Diego later in the season, Magic got the ball at midcourt and fired a pass right between two Clippers to forward Jim Chones. Chones was surprised to find the ball in his hands, but he put it into the basket. As he made his way back down the floor on defense, Chones shook his head in disbelief. Earvin seemed to know where the ball was and was going to be, and where his teammates were going to be as well.

Magic's enthusiasm helped the other Lakers. His

Magic learned that the pro game was a lot rougher than the college game. Here he fights for control of the ball against Marques Johnson of the Milwaukee Bucks.

"cheerleading style" rubbed off on them. They all started to enjoy the game more.

Midway in the season, Coach McKinney was injured when he fell off a bicycle he was riding near his home. His assistant coach, Paul Westhead, took over. A former teacher of English literature, Westhead was well liked by the players. His style of coaching was different from McKinney's, but it was a style the team could respect. By mid-March the Lakers had made the Western Conference playoffs. They went on to beat the Phoenix Suns in the semi-finals and to face the Seattle Supersonics for the conference championship.

In 1978, the Seattle Supersonics had knocked the Lakers out of the playoffs in the first round. The next year, they had beaten them in the conference semifinals and then gone on to win the NBA championship. The Lakers felt it was their turn now. They beat the Sonics four games to one to win the Western Conference title.

Meanwhile, back in the East, the Boston Celtics had been defeated by the Philadelphia 76ers in the Eastern Division playoff series. The season was over for Larry Bird, the other famous NBA rookie, but he was named NBA Rookie of the Year. Many people thought that Magic played well enough to at least share that award with Bird. Still, if it was a choice between playing in the NBA championship series and winning Rookie of the Year, there was no doubt about which he would choose. He wouldn't change places with Larry Bird for anything.

In the NBA championship series between the Lakers and the Philadelphia 76ers, the first two games were played in Los Angeles. The Lakers won the first, 109–102. Abdul-Jabbar had a game-high 33 points and 14 rebounds. Johnson had 16 points, 10 assists, and nine rebounds. They lost the second, 107–104. The Lakers packed up to go to Philadelphia, where they had not won a game since 1975. Happily they broke that record in the very first game, winning 111–101; but they lost the next, 105–102.

The Lakers won the fifth game at home, 108–103, but the win cost them their star center. In the third period, Kareem Abdul-Jabbar went up for a rebound, got tangled up with other players, and crashed to the floor injuring his left ankle. He sat out the remaining minutes of the period. The score was close, and with the series tied, this game was a must for the Lakers. If they lost, they would go back to Philadelphia down one game, and nobody wanted to do that. Kareem went back in and helped his team win, scoring 14 of his 40 points playing with a sprained left ankle. He even made a three-point play with 33 seconds left to break a 103–103 tie.

Now that the Lakers were one game ahead in the series, the managers and coaches decided that they could afford to keep Abdul-Jabbar out of the next game in Philadelphia. He could rest his ankle for a couple of days. If the Lakers lost the sixth game in Philadelphia, he would still be able to play in the seventh and final game in Los Angeles.

With Abdul-Jabbar out of the lineup, Coach West-head had to make some big changes. The reserve forward, Michael Cooper, would start as guard with Norm Nixon. On defense, forward Jim Chones would play center, and Magic Johnson would move from guard to forward. But on offense, Chones would return to his forward position and Magic would play center. A lot of people thought Westhead was crazy and said that the former English teacher had "read too many books."

Meanwhile, the rest of the team knew nothing about these decisions. They were not told until they arrived at the airport for the flight to Philadelphia. Earvin Johnson was used to being switched around from position to position on teams. But center? He had not played center since his days at Everett High. And he had never been called upon to fill the shoes of a player like Kareem Abdul-Jabbar.

The Lakers were quiet and thoughtful as they boarded the plane to Philadelphia on the afternoon of May 15. Their big guy wasn't with them. They were not afraid of losing without him, or at least they told themselves they were not. But it would be hard to make up for the loss of his per game average of 33.4 points, 13.6 rebounds, and 4.6 blocked shots. And it didn't seem right not to have Abdul-Jabbar with them after all that the team had been through together.

Earvin Johnson was positive that the Lakers would win in Philadelphia. They had to do it for Kareem. He took his responsibility for that effort very seriously. He asked to wear Abdul-Jabbar's number, 33. If he was going to play in Kareem's position on court, he felt he ought to wear the big man's number. He was allowed to do that. The same went for Kareem's seat on the plane. Kareem always took the first seat in the first row on the left side of the plane. So when the team boarded the plane for Philadelphia, there was Magic sitting in that seat. If he was going to be Kareem-for-a-day, he was going to do it right.

The Lakers surprised the 76ers at the opening tip-off. Instead of Jim Chones as jumping center, there was the rookie Magic Johnson. And not only was he there, but he was giggling! He just couldn't believe he was at center. The 76ers won the tip, but the Lakers scored the first seven points before the 76ers finally got started. The 76ers caught up, and the lead changed hands often. By halftime the score was 60-all.

In the Lakers' locker room, there was agreement that they were playing well without Kareem, but they also knew they could do better. In fact, why not go for it? Magic decided to be team cheerleader as never before.

The Lakers were out for blood as they returned for the start of the second half. Magic had the first field goal, and the team went on to score the first 14 points of the period, cheered on by their teammate, Magic. He handed out high-five handshakes, hugged any Laker within reach, jumped wildly, and raised a clenched fist to the ceiling every time they made a good play. By the end of the period, the Lakers had a 10-point lead. The 76ers rallied in the fourth period and three times got within one basket of a tie. With five minutes remaining, the Lakers launched a shooting barrage, and when the buzzer sounded, the scoreboard showed 123–107. The Los Angeles Lakers were the champions of the NBA!

The people who watched the series had thought all along that the series MVP would be Abdul-Jabbar if the Lakers won, or Julius Erving if the 76ers did. But after Magic's performance in that sixth game, there was no question that he was the MVP. Coach Westhead called him "Mr. Opportunity." Philadelphia Coach Billy Cunningham said, "If you ask me to compare him with Larry Bird, I'd have to take Johnson." Magic was happier than he had ever been before in his life. But he had not forgotten his hero. When the first microphone was stuck in his face and the first television camera rolled into posi-

Magic played like a veteran in the championship series between the Lakers and the Philadelphia 76ers, fighting under the boards against the 76ers' Darryl Dawkins.

tion, he looked right into it. He grinned his famous grin and said to Jabbar, "Big Fella, I did it for you. I know your ankle hurts, but I want you to get up and dance."

Back in Los Angeles, Kareem, who had sweated through the whole televised game, broke up with laughter. Later, he was asked if he minded not being in on the victory he'd worked so hard for all season. "Not at all," he said. "I was meant to be here, and Earvin was meant to have that game."

Magic Johnson was the hottest news item in sports. No matter where he went, he was surrounded by press and fans. He signed contracts to do advertisements for 7-Up, Converse sneakers, and Spalding basketballs. But he kept his promise to his mother and went home to Lansing to take summer school courses at MSU. There, he was greeted as a returning hero, even though the MSU basketball team had not done very well that year without him.

It was a golden time for 20-year-old Earvin Johnson. He was young, he was rich, he was getting paid to play the game he loved. He was winning at the pro game just as he had in high school and college. In fact, he had won so often that his coach worried that he didn't have a very realistic idea about the game. As Westhead put it, "Magic thinks every season goes like this. You play some games, win the title, and get named MVP."

Chapter 4

The 1980–1981 season began well for Magic. After 20 games, he was the team's leading scorer and second-best rebounder. Then, in November, he injured his left knee twice in the space of five days. Two days after that, in a game against Kansas City, something in his knee popped or cracked, and down to the floor he went. The cartilage in his knee was severely torn. He underwent surgery less than a week later. After that, he was in a cast for several weeks, and after the cast was off he had to exercise to get his knee and his whole body back in shape. Altogether, Magic missed 45 games.

He had never before been seriously injured, and it was a difficult time for him. Only years later did he see it as a "blessing in disguise." He explained in 1984, "It made me see that everything came fast and good and that it could easily be taken away just as fast."

Meanwhile, the Lakers were having a difficult time adjusting to the loss of Magic. Without him, they gave up five out of their next nine games. But then, led by

Abdul-Jabbar, they started to regroup and stayed alive in the NBA's Western Conference. If Magic came back healthy, they had a shot at their second NBA championship in a row.

Magic did come back healthy on March 1, 1981. After it was announced that he would return in a game against the New Jersey Nets that night, tickets for that game were sold out. Many fans wore buttons that said, "The Magic is Back." While his teammates were pleased by his recovery, they resented all the publicity and hoopla. After all, they had done quite well without him. And now they had to adjust again, this time to having him back on the team.

Magic and his teammates made the necessary adjustments. There were just 17 games remaining in the regular season, and they won eleven and made the Western Conference playoffs. They went on to play the Houston Rockets in the semifinals, but lost the series to Houston. Magic had the unhappy distinction of being the Laker who took, and missed, the final shot in the final game against the Rockets. Later, the Rockets lost to the Boston Celtics in the NBA championship series.

Magic had a hard time getting over that loss and his feeling that it had been his fault. But no one else blamed him. That last shot had been a gamble that hadn't paid off. The Lakers' managers and coaches did not blame him. In fact, three months after the championship series ended, team owner Jerry Buss signed Magic to the biggest contract to date in sports history.

Magic's original contract was not due to expire until 1984. But a new arrangement between owners and players in the NBA caused the Laker's owner to decide he could not wait that long to ensure that Magic would stay with the team. This new arrangement, called the right-of-first-refusal system, gave a player the chance to become a "free agent" when his contract expired. A free agent could move to any team he wanted, and other teams could offer as much as they wanted for his services. Buss was certain that in 1984 other teams would offer Magic big sums of money. So, Buss offered Magic an "extension" to his present contract, that provided for a huge sum of money. Beginning in 1984, when Magic's current contract ended, he would receive one million dollars a year for 25 years!

Clearly, he couldn't play for 25 more years. What that contract meant was that Buss wanted Magic with the Lakers as a coach or general manager or in some other job after his playing days were over. It meant that the Lakers' management saw Magic Johnson as a crowd-pleaser and a seller of tickets. Magic's teammates did not like that contract at all. Kareem Abdul-Jabbar earned good money, but his contract was short term.

During the 1981–1982 season, some people started asking if the contract made Magic a part of management. Eleven games into the season, the Lakers were at Salt Lake City playing the Utah Jazz. Magic and Coach Westhead argued about how the team's offense should be run. Magic told reporters that he wanted to be traded. The next day, Westhead was fired. Many people wanted to know who was running the team.

Assistant Coach Pat Riley, who replaced Westhead, does not believe that Magic was really to blame. Other Lakers were unhappy with Westhead's offensive strategy, but none of those teammates defended Magic in public.

For several weeks, Magic was booed everywhere the

Lakers went. He finished fifth among guards for the West All-Star team. It was the only time, except for his injury season, that he failed to make the starting lineup. He was more depressed than ever before. He kept his famous smile on his face, but it was like a mask—there was no sparkle behind it.

But he did not let his emotions affect his playing. Under Coach Pat Riley, the Lakers' offense did improve. They swept the Phoenix Suns 4–0 in the Western Conference championships and went on to win the NBA championship against the Philadelphia 76ers. Still, for much of that season and post-season, basketball had become a job for Earvin Johnson. The fun was gone.

By the time the next season started, Magic's natural enthusiasm had returned. He was more mature, with a greater sense of reality. But the Lakers' 1982–1983 season was a tough one. The team was plagued by injuries. Magic dislocated his right index finger and missed a month. Other Lakers had injuries of various kinds. They made it all the way to the championship series, but in that series against the Philadelphia 76ers, the Lakers played without guard Norm Nixon and forwards Bob McAdoo and James Worthy. The 76ers took the series in four straight games.

Norm Nixon was traded away after that season. Earvin was sorry to see him go. Though he knew that many players got traded all around the NBA during their careers, he wished the Lakers could be different. He, for one, wanted to stay with the Lakers forever, and he wanted to play with the same teammates.

The 1983–1984 season began as a fine one for Magic and the Lakers. By February, he was averaging 14.4 assists and matching NBA passing records such as the

Magic starts his glide for a lay-up against the Golden State Warriors.

greatest number of assists in the first quarter of a game. Every bit of his old enthusiasm was back.

As the season wore on, Magic had good reason to be enthusiastic. The Lakers were performing extremely well together, and Magic was playing some of his best basketball ever. Without Norm Nixon, the team had come to rely heavily on him for rebounds and assists. He met that need, and more. At the end of the season the Lakers were again in the Western Conference championship playoffs, their fifth year in a row. During those playoffs against the Phoenix Suns, Magic had 24 assists in a single game, the highest ever in an NBA post-season contest. For the fourth time in five years, they were the Western Conference champs.

In the NBA championship playoffs, they faced the Boston Celtics. It was the first time since they had both entered pro basketball that Magic Johnson and Larry Bird were opponents in a championship series. The press, and just about everyone else, remembered their old rivalry and really played it up this time around. But no wonder. Most people considered the two players the best in basketball. Not since 1969 had the two best players in the game been matched in a championship series. In that year, the Lakers played Boston, and centers Wilt Chamberlain and Bill Russell squared off against each other. The Celtics had won.

The Johnson-Bird contest was different from the one between Chamberlain and Russell. Johnson and Bird played different positions. Johnson was a ball-handler and playmaker. Bird was a scorer and rebounder. But the comparisons were made anyway. Once again, sportswriters drew up charts of statistics. These charts showed that Bird scored more points and pulled down more rebounds. They also showed that Johnson had more assists. But they showed, too, that both were extremely well-rounded players who could do everything. That was really why they were compared. Both Johnson and Bird tried not to pay attention to the comparisons, but they could not help being affected by them.

The first two games were played in Boston because the Celtics had a better regular-season record. The Lakers won the first. In the second, the score was tied at 113-all with 13 seconds left on the game clock. Magic brought the ball down the court. He wanted to get it to Bob McAdoo, but he lost track of time. By the time he passed to McAdoo, there was nothing the Laker forward could do. The game went into overtime, and the Celtics won.

In Game 3 in Los Angeles, the Lakers won in a 33-point blowout of the Celtics. In Game 4 they led 113–108, with 56 seconds left, but Boston's center Robert Parish made a three-point play. Kareem Abdul-Jabbar committed his sixth foul, and Larry Bird made two free throws. With 16 seconds remaining, Magic had the ball and tried to get it to James Worthy. But Parish stepped in and stole the ball away. The game went into overtime. Kareem Abdul-Jabbar had fouled out, and without his defense, Larry Bird had no trouble going inside to make baskets. With 35 seconds left, Magic was fouled, but he missed both free throws. In that game, he had a triple double (statistics in double figures)—20 points, 17 assists, 11 rebounds. But what stood out in memory were the pass he threw away and the two free throws he missed.

For Magic, the whole championship series seemed to go that way. Mistakes in crucial moments haunted him.

As the highest-paid member of the team, Magic felt sometimes as if he was alone on the court. When the team lost, he blamed himself.

He had set a playoff record for most assists, with 95, and had averaged 18 points a game. But he had also set one for most turnovers. He admitted that for the first time he had been "too cautious."

His friends Isiah Thomas of the Detroit Pistons and Mark Aguirre of the Dallas Mavericks sat up all night with him after the final loss. They tried to talk him out of blaming himself for everything. His coach reminded the public, and him, that after Norm Nixon had been traded, the team had relied on him to do too much and had put too much pressure on him. But Magic could not get over feeling responsible. "It's gonna be a long summer," he said with a sigh.

Chapter 5

The one thing that gave Magic Johnson pleasure at that time was a new house he had bought in Bel Air, an exclusive section near Los Angeles. It was still so new that it didn't even have furniture in it, but often at night Earvin would go there and sit on the floor in the dark and think about how he would decorate it. It was big—five bedrooms—and while he was a big man, he knew he couldn't use them all. So he decided to "reserve" some of the bedrooms and name them for the people he wanted to visit. It would be like a fancy hotel. He named one room the Christine Room, after his mother, and another the Isiah Room, for his friend Isiah Thomas of the Detroit Pistons.

None of these people visited all the time, and it was a very large house for a bachelor. But Magic Johnson still was not ready to get married. He had been dating a girl named Cookie Kelly, a department store manager in Toledo, Ohio, for about seven years. But he also dated other girls. He was afraid of making such a big commitment as marriage. It seemed to him that he needed all his concentration for the game of basketball. And especially after that loss to the Celtics in the 1984 championship series, Magic Johnson felt he needed all his concentration just to get over that loss. "We made five mistakes that cost us that series," he later said, "and I contributed to three of them."

He could not seem to get the championship series losses out of his mind. The press did not help. Reporters were hard on him and wrote that he had "choked" in crucial moments. They wrote about how he had failed against his rival, Larry Bird. It also did not help matters that some of those reporters remembered that the upcoming 1984–1985 season was to be the start of that historic $25-million, 25-year contract that Magic had signed with the Lakers.

Even when the 1984–1985 season started, Magic had failed to put the previous season's losses behind him. He did not smile much anymore, and especially not on the basketball court. Some people were getting impatient with him for taking it all so personally, for not being mature enough to put the loss behind him and go on. Boston's Kevin McHale called him "Tragic Johnson."

Magic played well that season, as did his teammates, but by early 1985 the winds of change seemed to be in the air. Kareem Abdul-Jabbar announced that the 1985–1986 season would be his last. Not long afterward, Magic announced that he did not expect to play more than five or six more years. His contract with the Lakers had been reworked so that he would receive one million dollars a year for the next ten years, covering a playing career that would end when he was 35. (The rest would be paid to him after he retired as a player.) But Magic

Magic crashes into Larry Smith of Golden State. By the 1984-1985 season he was beginning to wonder if he could play the rough pro game for many more years.

didn't think he could manage the fast-paced Lakers' game for ten years. He had lost 15 pounds the previous season doing all that running and playing 35+ minutes of every 48-minute game.

Still, as the season wore on, his old enthusiasm began to return. Sportswriters began to say kind things about him again. A few even repeated that he was the best player in the game. By the time the Lakers met the Denver Nuggets for the Western Conference championship, most observers had decided that the magic was back. And after the Lakers beat the Nuggets and faced the Celtics again for the NBA championship, Magic himself was back in the groove, not just in his playing but in his heart.

So was Kareem Abdul-Jabbar. He had not been exactly pleased about the 1984 loss to the Celtics either. He, too, was determined to win the championship back. And, knowing that his playing days were nearly over, he wanted this championship as much as Magic did.

The Celtics won the first game, and Abdul-Jabbar played poorly in it. But both he and the Lakers roared back to win Game 2. By Game 3, Abdul-Jabbar was hurling all of his 7-foot two-inch body after loose balls and dribbling the length of the floor to make a sky-hook. In that game, with another one of his famous sky-hooks, he broke Jerry West's all-time NBA playoff scoring record.

Meanwhile, Earvin Johnson was playing some of his best team basketball ever. His teammates and his coach knew that he was the reason why forwards James Worthy and Bob McAdoo, not to mention Kareem Abdul-Jabbar, were scoring so well. He also made a basket when the opportunity presented itself. In some ways, he was grateful that so much of the limelight was on Kareem because he felt less pressure. And when, after a hard-fought series, the Lakers beat the Celtics for the NBA championship, no one was happier than Magic Johnson. Some of the pressure had been taken off him that year; he really felt part of the team again.

That summer, Magic Johnson and Larry Bird did two television commercials together, and they got to know each other for the first time. They did not talk about basketball very much, except to agree that they would probably be retiring within a year or so of each other because the game was so physical and neither believed he could last more than a few years longer. They talked mostly about how they considered themselves "small-town guys" who wanted to lead simple lives once they retired. After all those years of public rivalry, both men enjoyed their private talks at a time when they could relax and there were no serious axes to grind. Both the Lakers and the Celtics had won NBA championships in the years since Johnson and Bird had joined the pro game. And in the two championship series in which they had been matched, each man's team had won once.

Earvin Johnson was feeling more grown-up. He got engaged to Cookie Kelly, but he did not want to get married until after Kareem Abdul-Jabbar's last basketball season.

For the Lakers, the 1985–1986 season got off to the best start in the history of the team. Magic, however, missed the first game of the season because of a case of shingles, a painful virus that infects the nervous system. A month later, he suffered a sprained finger. Two months after that, it was a bruised knee. No wonder he believed he could not play more than a few more seasons.

Even so, in the games he did play, he piled up some

impressive statistics. By the end of April he was making 66 percent of his shots from the floor and was averaging 18.3 points per game and 15.5 assists. Also, he was as enthusiastic as he had been in his rookie year. Part of the reason may have been that it was supposed to be Kareem Abdul-Jabbar's last season. Part may have been his awareness that he himself might not play many more seasons.

The Lakers beat the Seattle Supersonics in the semifinals of the Western Conference championship. But in the finals, the Lakers were stunned by the Dallas

Magic tried to play every game as if it was a championship game. Here, he passes against the Milwaukee Bucks in a game that saw the Lakers come from behind to win.

Mavericks. As a result, their summer began early that year. It was the first time they had not been in the NBA championship series in four years (since 1982, when they were eliminated in the playoffs by the Houston Rockets). They could only watch as the Boston Celtics beat the Mavericks.

But this summer, Magic Johnson didn't feel responsible for the loss. It had been a team season, and all the players had shared equally in the wins and the losses. Kareem Abdul-Jabbar decided not to retire, and Magic Johnson was glad of that. There wouldn't be so many adjustments to make that fall.

Magic spent the summer staying busy. He had lots of things to do. He and Isiah Thomas owned a radio station in Denver, Colorado. He was taking summer courses at MSU. He had been sponsoring a kids' baseball team in East Lansing ever since he had left MSU for the NBA. Earlier that year, he had decided to sponsor an all-star basketball game in August to raise money for the United Negro College Fund. He called 20 of the NBA's top players and invited them to play. But as the time approached, he found that most of them were unavailable. Even Larry Bird, who had promised to take part in the game, suddenly found out that the Celtics' management did not want him to participate. But Bird was determined to live up to his promise, and he did. For his part, Magic made sure they played on the same team. The game did take place in August as planned, and it raised $300,000 for the United Negro College Fund.

That same month, Magic Johnson broke a promise when he called off his engagement to Cookie Kelly. "I can't get married now," is all he would say. "Not while I'm still married to basketball."

Magic runs around Rod Higgins of the Chicago Bulls.

During that summer, the Lakers' management decided they had to do something to erase the indignity of their loss to the Houston Rockets in the Western Conference finals. They talked about trading forward James Worthy to the Dallas Mavericks in exchange for Mark Aguirre, Magic's friend. But the Dallas coach would not agree to the trade. It was rumored that Magic was behind the idea of the trade, and he realized that Worthy might believe the rumors. He called Worthy, and they talked. Neither one will say what they talked about. But that fall James Worthy showed that he belonged with the Lakers. The 1986–1987 season would be his best since he joined the pros five years earlier out of North Carolina.

Chapter 6

The 1986–1987 season was also the best ever for the Laker team as a whole. In the regular season, they had a record of 65–17, the best in the NBA and the best for the Lakers in years. They had an even better record in the playoffs, barrelling past the Golden State Warriors four games to one in the Western Conference semifinals and sweeping the Seatle Supersonics 4–0 in the finals. In fact, it took them such a short time to eliminate their opponents that they had several days to rest and to wonder whom they would be up against in the playoffs.

The Eastern Conference finals matched the Detroit Pistons against the Boston Celtics, and Magic had mixed feelings about whom he wanted to win. His friend Isiah Thomas was on the Detroit team, and naturally he wanted his friend to win. He did not even mind the idea of playing against Isiah in the championship series. But Magic also wanted a chance to play against the Lakers' archrival, the Celtics, in another championship series, and that meant rooting for a Boston win over Detroit.

As it turned out, the Celtics beat Detroit, setting the stage for the rematch. Magic looked forward to it and was confident that the Lakers would win this time.

But in the meantime, Magic had an individual victory that meant as much, if not more, to him. Two days after the Lakers beat Seattle for the Western Conference championship, Earvin "Magic" Johnson was named the Most Valuable Player in the NBA for the 1986–1987 season.

He deserved it. During the regular season, he had averaged a career-high 23.9 points per game and led the

Magic at Logan Airport in Boston. Being a pro basketball player means spending a good part of your life on the road.

league in assists with 12.2. He was credited with inspiring his team to the 65–17 won-lost record that was the best in the league. He was only the third guard in NBA history to win the award. At a news conference following the announcement that he had won, Magic said, "I'd like to thank Larry Bird for having a slightly off year." But he was joking. He believed that he had won the MVP award entirely on his own.

The Lakers were heavy favorites to win the championship. The Celtics had struggled hard to beat their opponents in the semifinals and finals of the Eastern Conference. Several Celtics were playing hurt, and they had only a couple days to rest between beating Detroit and starting the championship series against the Lakers. And because the Lakers had the better regular-season record, the first two games of the series would be played in Los Angeles.

The Lakers won those two games handily. In the opener, they won 126–113; they took the second 141–122. The home-court advantage helped, of course, but they also played better basketball than the Boston team. The Celtics could only look forward to the fact that the next three games would be played at Boston Garden. There, the old, uneven parquet floor and the lack of air conditioning, not to mention the Boston fans, were famous as being as hard to beat as the Celtics themselves. The Celtics had won all but two of their last 96 games there since beating the Lakers in Game 6 of the 1985 finals. Of course, those two losses had been at the hands of the Lakers.

In Boston, the Celtics did win the third game of the series, 109–103, and for most of Game 4 it looked as if they were going to even up the series at two wins apiece. They led from the opening minutes of the game and by

55–47 at the half. Among the Lakers, only Magic was shooting well. In the third period the Celtics were ahead by 16 points. In the fourth quarter, the Lakers, led by Magic, came back and managed to tie the game at 95-all. But the Celtics came back to life and opened up another lead. As the game clock wound down, the Lakers came to within a point, but there were only about eight seconds left. Then Magic took charge. He made a "junior sky-hook" (like Kareem's favorite shot, only from Magic's height of 6 feet nine inches, not Kareem's 7 feet two inches) with two seconds to go and put his team ahead by a point, 107–106. The Celtics were unable to score again before time ran out. The Celtics were stunned. They had needed to win that game.

Both teams now packed up and flew west to Los Angeles. For the Lakers, it was a homecoming; all the rest

Magic punches the ball away from Kevin McHale of the Celtics in the 1987 NBA championship series.

of the series games, however many there were, would be played on their home court. Odds-makers were betting on them to wrap up the series in the next game, but the Celtics were not about to lie down and be beaten. No NBA team had ever come back from a 3–1 deficit to win a championship series, but they were going to try. They won that fifth game in Los Angeles decisively, 123–108.

Suddenly, sportswriters started talking about what they called the Lakers' "longstanding weakness": their inability at times to stand the pressures of playing for the championship. The Celtics, by contrast, had almost always been able to overcome those pressures. People called this ability "courage" and questioned again if the Lakers had it.

Magic Johnson and his teammates decided that they had just as much courage as they needed. They proved it in the sixth game. After the Lakers established an early lead, the Celtics collected themselves and led during most of the first half. At intermission they had a five-point lead. Johnson had a poor first half, missing seven of nine shots and scoring only four points. James Worthy and Kareem Abdul-Jabbar were making their shots, but it was not enough to catch up to the Celtics. But when the Lakers came back after intermission, it was a whole new ballgame. Not only did they play superb defense, but they also got their fast break back. They were explosive. Early in the third period, James Worthy tipped a Celtic pass and dived toward the loose ball, bumping it toward the Lakers' basket. Magic was right there to retrieve it and, all alone, drove down the court for a slam dunk. From then on, led by Magic, the Lakers controlled the game, outscoring the Celtics 18–2 during the first seven minutes. By the end of the period, Magic had scored 14 points in just that one quarter. The Lakers won the game 106–93, and the championship series four games to two.

As the champagne flowed in the Lakers' locker room, Earvin "Magic" Johnson learned that he had been named championship series MVP for the third time in his pro career. With his earlier NBA Most Valuable Player award, not to mention the championship series win, this was a banner season for Magic Johnson. It was also his best, he said, because of his team: "This is the greatest team I've ever played on. This team can run,

Magic loves the game of basketball and intends to play it, and have fun at it, as long as he can.

shoot, rebound, hit from outside, can do it all. I've never played on a team that had everything before."

In the following 1987-88 season, the Lakers finished regular play with a record of 62-20 and clinched a play-off berth. Despite their record, the Lakers had a difficult time beating Utah and Dallas. After a grueling seven-game competition, the Lakers beat the Detroit Pistons 103-102 in the final game for the championship. They were now the first team in nineteen years to win two NBA championship titles back-to-back. Unlike others, the tough Pistons didn't surprise Magic. He acknowledged them as a new force saying, "It's no longer just L.A. and Boston in this league. Detroit is here. And here to stay."

After the season, Magic continued playing ball. For the third time he held his annual MidSummer Night's Magic Weekend Extravaganza to raise money for the United Negro College Fund. The two-day event, featuring an all-star basketball game, raised $650,000.

Between 1980 and 1988 the Lakers appeared in all but two championship games and won five titles. As a team the Lakers were ready to go for another victory, their momentum carrying them into their good start of the 1988-89 season.

Earvin Johnson knew very well that basketball wasn't all playing and winning. The impending retirement of Kareem Abdul-Jabbar put the spotlight even more intensely on Magic. Basketball was and would continue to be a struggle and heartache as well as fun and joy. But he didn't regret it. In fact, he was thankful. He was also thankful that he still loved the game and that he could look forward to a few more years of playing it. He wanted to have a good time during those years.

Chapter 7

Over the next three seasons, Magic did have a good time. When Kareem Abdul-Jabbar retired after a long and illustrious career, Magic became the undisputed leader of the Lakers team. Coach Pat Riley also retired, although he would later change his mind and coach the New York Knickerbockers. Even though the Lakers replaced Riley with a new coach, Magic took on a lot of responsibility.

Magic was like a floor coach at games, talking his teammates through plays in a voice loud enough that members of the press, not to mention the opposing team, could hear. Once in a while a reporter would ask him if he didn't worry that his opponents would know what the next play was going to be. Magic would answer that if you did something right, it didn't matter who knew it was coming.

He was a leader off the court as well. During the 1987 NBA finals against the Boston Celtics, the Lakers won the first two games. After the second win, guard Michael Cooper spent what Magic thought was too much time talking to reporters. He worried that his teammates were getting too cocky and might not work hard in the next game. So he whispered to Cooper to end the interview. Cooper kept on talking. Magic then tapped him on the shoulder and told him to end the interview, Now! Cooper smiled and shrugged and said to the reporters, "Well, you heard him."

Only a player who enjoyed the respect of his teammates could have gotten away with that. Magic did have their respect. The other Lakers knew that whatever he did was for the good of the team.

The team did not fare as well in the early 1990s as it had in the 1980s. Magic missed Coach Riley. After the Chicago Bulls defeated the Lakers in four straight games in the 1991 finals, a disappointed Magic told reporters that he was already planning for life after basketball. As the seasons passed, time began to tell on Magic—at least a little. He had turned thirty on August 14, 1989, and some sportswriters thought he was slowing down a bit. But Magic had never depended on acrobatics or speed. His greatest asset was his court sense—his seemingly uncanny ability to know where every other player was and where they were about to go. This ability did not diminish with age. In fact, it increased. And Earvin Johnson continued to make magic on the court, and to enjoy the game.

He also continued to have fun playing the role of a basketball star. Everywhere he went, he was mobbed by fans. Young people wanted his autograph, and he nearly always obliged. Reporters wanted interviews, and he took the time to talk to them. Charities wanted him to make appearances to help them raise money; he rarely turned such an invitation down, and raised thousands of dollars for various causes. Women wanted to be around him—lots of women—and Magic tried hard not to disappoint them either.

Magic made no secret of the fact that he liked women, and

Magic shows his uncanny ability to know where every other player was with a quick bounce-pass.

he liked the idea that so many women wanted to be with him. He was no different from many professional athletes. At home and on the road, they are approached by women who want to be seen with them, to be taken out to dinner, to be invited to a game. They call the players' hotel rooms. They send pictures of themselves with notes that say, "When you're in my town, give me a call." There is one story of a woman who invites players to her home if they will give her an autographed pair of basketball sneakers. She is rumored to have a collection of hundreds of pairs of autographed sneakers in her closet.

Sex is expected, and many of the women do not use any form of birth control. Some women feel that if they get pregnant by a professional athlete, they will be set for life. The player might either marry them or pay money to take care of them and the baby. Magic fathered a child out of wedlock. Although he did not marry the woman, he acknowledged the baby boy, who was named Andre, as his son and took care of him and his mother. Magic and the other professional athletes who went out with these women did not stop to think that it was wrong to sleep around, or that it was dangerous. The women were part of the glamorous role they played.

Magic sometimes felt guilty about stringing his long-time girlfriend Cookie along for so many years. He realized it was unfair to her to keep putting off marriage. After he turned thirty, he began thinking seriously about settling down and starting a family. But he didn't act on those thoughts for another two years.

Then, in the late summer of 1991, Cookie announced that she was pregnant, and Magic realized he could not stall any longer. On September 14, 1991, one month after he turned thirty-two, he and Cookie were married in Magic's hometown of Lansing, Michigan. Magic would miss the bachelor's life, but he liked the idea of being a family man and looked forward to the birth of the baby.

It was going to be a big year ahead. The Lakers had been invited to Paris to play in the McDonald's Open. Then the 1991-1992 season would begin, during which the team would have to work hard if they didn't want to repeat the disappointing defeat of the 1991 finals. Magic and Cookie's baby would be born in June, and with any luck the team would be in the championship playoffs at just about the same time. What if he became a father and his team won another championship in the same month? And the fun would not stop there. In the summer of 1992 Magic was going to play in the Summer Olympics with the first U.S. All-Star Olympic team featuring professional athletes.

The Lakers went to Paris to play in the McDonald's Open and crowds mobbed Magic everywhere he went. He was a real ambassador of basketball. Magic had his picture taken in front of the Eiffel Tower, his smile bigger than ever.

Back in the United States, the new NBA season began. But Magic missed the first three games because of the flu. Or so everyone thought. He had flu-like symptoms and stayed in bed so he could join his team before he missed too many more games.

In the meantime, Magic had a big business deal in mind. Although he is worth a lot of money, he needed to borrow some more to close the deal. So he approached the Lakers and asked for a loan. Lakers management wanted to help their star player, but business was business. To secure the loan, they wanted to take out an insurance policy on his life.

Before granting the policy, the insurance company insisted that Magic have a medical examination and some tests. Magic had the examination. He thought it was a routine matter. Then he learned that the insurance company would not grant the policy. On October 25, 1991, Magic Johnson learned that a test for the HIV virus done on his blood had come back positive. He had the HIV virus.

HIV is short for human immunodeficiency virus (im-yuh-noh-di-FISH-en-see). It is the virus that causes AIDS, or acquired immune deficiency syndrome. When someone suffers from the HIV virus, the immune system in their body does not work the way it is supposed to. Instead of fighting the disease, the immune system allows infections and diseases to hurt the body. These infections or diseases are called "AIDS-defining" illnesses. They include a cancer called Kaposi's sarcoma, a type of pneumonia, and several blood-related infections. A person with one or more of these illnesses is said to have AIDS. People infected with the HIV virus may feel healthy for months or even years, but there is no known cure for AIDS. Experts at the Center for Disease Control have projected that about 99 percent of those infected with HIV will eventually die of AIDS.

A few drugs have been found to be effective in slowing down the AIDS virus. Two of these drugs are AZT (azidothymidine) and ddI (dideoxyinosine). But, these drugs only slow the AIDS diseases, they do not stop or cure them. Doctors hope that with early treatment with AZT and ddI, and with even more powerful drugs that have yet to be developed, it will take longer and longer before AIDS symptoms occur and prevent some infected people from ever becoming ill.

At first, Magic could not believe he had the HIV virus. He felt fine. Anyway, HIV was something that gay men and drug users had, not an athlete in top shape who is not gay. The Laker's doctor Michael Mellman hoped that Magic did not have the HIV virus either. He ordered another test, maybe the first test was wrong and the second test would come back negative. But he told Magic that he should not hold out too much hope.

Magic decided to tell his family that he had tested positive for the HIV virus. He needed to talk to somebody about what was happening to him. He did not want to keep anything from them. Cookie and his parents were stunned. Magic was afraid Cookie might not be able to handle it and offered to leave her. She would not hear of it. "She's a strong woman," he said later. "I was smart to marry her." The thing that worried Cookie most was the fear that the baby was infected. Magic was concerned about both Cookie and the baby. They decided that Cookie should have a test to make sure she and the baby were not also infected with the HIV virus. Fortunately, they tested negative.

On November 6, 1991, Magic's second blood test came back positive as well. There had been no mistake. Often one of the first signs that someone has contracted the HIV virus are symptoms that are like those of flu: fevers, chills, sweats, and very high temperature. Flu-like symptoms had caused Magic to miss the first three Laker games of the season. Many newly infected people also develop a rash that covers their body but disappears after a few days. Magic had not developed any rash. After flu-like symptoms and/or a rash, there may be no further symptoms for years until the symptoms of AIDS itself occur. By that time, the HIV virus may have destroyed many of the cells that make up the immune system.

Although there is no evidence showing that playing strenuous sports has any effect on the progress of the HIV virus or the onset of AIDS, Dr. Mellman advised Magic to quit basketball. He said the strain of playing might damage his immune system. He would become sick sooner than if he quit playing.

69

For Magic there was no question about it. He wanted to stay healthy as long as he could. He wanted to see his baby grow. He would quit basketball. That night he called his close friends—Isiah Thomas, Larry Bird, former Laker coach Pat Riley, and Arsenio Hall, the late-night talk show host. He called friends back in Lansing. He wanted everyone who was close to him to hear the news from him, not on the radio or TV. He had done a lot of thinking about what was going to happen. He wanted to handle it as a man, to be strong, and not to let it get him down, and he would need his friends. He asked them to be there for him. They all said they would.

The following afternoon Magic walked into the Laker locker room to tell his teammates. They had already heard rumors, but they couldn't believe them until they heard the news from Magic himself. "Breaking the news to my teammates was the most emotional experience of this entire ordeal," Magic later wrote in *Sports Illustrated*. "Everyone was crying, including me." But Magic did not cry long. He wiped his eyes and told his teammates they had to stay strong for him. Seeing the way he was handling the most devastating news of his life, his teammates knew they had to be brave, too.

Now Magic had to tell the public. The Lakers management had called a press conference at the Great Western Forum for later that afternoon. Kareem Abdul-Jabbar was on hand to support Magic, along with the members of the Laker team. Magic, dressed in a suit and tie, stepped to the microphones and got right to the point: "Because of the HIV virus I have obtained, I will have to retire from the Lakers today," he said.

The news made front-page headlines and was the lead story on the nightly TV news for several days. Few people in America, or in the world, who heard the news failed to be shocked and saddened. Even those who didn't especially follow sports knew who Magic Johnson was. Over the years his big smile and easy manner had made him friends he did not even know he had. It was as if everybody had just learned that their close friend had AIDS. Millions of people were sad.

The first reactions were of disbelief. How could Magic Johnson have AIDS? People who had never really thought about AIDS before suddenly realized that if it could happen to Magic it could happen to anyone. More than one professional athlete told reporters that they were going to get tested for

Magic discusses his retirement with reporters after he tells the world that he has the HIV virus.

AIDS. Many young men and women who had refused to use condoms decided they had better change their minds. Magic's news did more to get the word out that AIDS is a dangerous disease than all of the public service announcements that had been warning people put together. AIDS hotlines around the country were flooded with calls.

Magic understood that reaction. He also saw a way to use his disease in a positive manner. He would work to fight AIDS by getting the word out that the best protection from AIDS was safe sex—using condoms and being careful about choosing your partners.

The very next day, in fact, Magic made a special guest appearance on the "Arsenio Hall Show," which was broadcast that night. He was wasting no time in getting his safe sex message out. At the same time, he sought to reassure his fans. "You don't have to run from me like, 'Oh-oh, here comes Magic,'" he said at one point. He also said, "You don't have to feel sorry for me because if I die tomorrow I've had the greatest life."

For most people, after they got over the initial shock at hearing the news, the next feeling was admiration for Magic Johnson. He had just heard he had the HIV virus, and he was talking about how he could help others. Sports writers and editorial writers were full of praise. Companies like Converse athletic shoes, Nintendo games, and Kentucky Fried Chicken, issued statements of support. Magic was a spokesman for their products. Several companies announced that they were planning HIV-awareness campaigns around him.

Many agreed with Dr. Michael Mellmann that Magic was a "modern-day hero." But after the news settled in, some people began to take a second look at the hero image. After all, Magic Johnson had gotten the HIV virus because he had slept around, and he had slept around so much that he didn't even know who had given him the virus. Who was he to hold up as a role model to young people? How could he go around talking about safe sex when he had not bothered to practice it himself?

Magic's response was disarming. He didn't get angry or defensive. In a *Newsweek* article he said his critics were right. "You always thought you were a person who set a good example," he admitted. "Then, all of a sudden—boom. But I

Magic appears on the *Arsenio Hall Show* and discusses AIDS with his good friend Arsenio.

understand. Hey, it's me. And I did it. So, I pray more, and I ask God to give me more strength because I see He's got a mission for me, to help make society aware and to make society care."

The negative editorials did not last long. Few people were unwilling to forgive Magic. After all, he was being so open and honest. He never seemed to ask, "Why me?" He wasn't bitter. And after all, he was paying the price for his carelessness. Unlike Kareem Abdul-Jabbar, he would never have a chance to be a "grand old man of basketball," piling up ever more impressive career totals with each season. The time of his retirement was not his to choose; it had been chosen for him. And unless a cure for AIDS was discovered in the next few years, he might not live to old age.

Although Magic had no symptoms of AIDS, his doctors started him on AZT in the hope that early treatment could slow down the destructive action of the HIV virus. Magic welcomed the treatments. He intended to fight the virus and beat it. At the same time, he intended to fight the disease around the nation. "It's my job," he explained, "to help us all understand that the disease is bigger than we think. There are more than one million people in the U.S. who are infected with the AIDS virus but who don't know it, because they refuse to get tested."

The president of the United States agreed. President George Bush thought Magic Johnson could be a powerful role model in the fight against AIDS. He appointed Magic to the National Commission on AIDS. Magic accepted the appointment. But before Magic did anything else, he decided to take Cookie for a vacation in Hawaii. The past few days had been hard even on a man who was accustomed to the spotlight, and especially hard on a woman who was not. Magic needed time to walk on the beach and think. He managed to do that, in between hugs from passersby who recognized him and wanted to tell him they loved him.

AIDS is still a very frightening disease, and people are terrified of catching it. Most people are afraid to touch anyone with the HIV virus, fearing they will somehow catch it. Though many people were not afraid to touch him, even Magic Johnson ran into the prejudice that many other HIV positive people face.

Although he had retired from the NBA, he still hoped to be able to be part of the U.S. Olympic all-star basketball team in Barcelona, Spain, in the summer of 1992. For more than two months after he announced he had the HIV virus, no one publicly suggested he should not try to play in the Olympics if he felt well enough. Then, in January, a medical officer with the Australian Olympic Committee said he would recommend that his team not play Olympic basketball if Magic Johnson were on the court.

The medical officer, Dr. Brian Sando, explained that there was a slight possibility that Magic could infect another player. If Magic were hurt and bleeding, and if he came in contact with another player who was bleeding, his blood might get into the open wound of the other player. In a rough-and-tumble game like basketball, that type of contact could occur.

The doctor's comments made headlines, and were quickly rebutted not only by U.S. doctors but also by senior Australian officials. While some members of the Australian basketball team expressed concern about the risks they faced if they played against Magic, Australian officials hastened to assure the world that the Australian team would not boycott the Summer Olympics. The Olympic organizing committee in Barcelona, Spain, reviewed the matter and found no reason to prevent Magic from playing.

In the midst of the controversy, Magic Johnson was elected to the NBA All-Star Team. He was the fourth-leading vote-getter among Western Conference players and seventh over all in the votes that are cast by basketball fans each year. Magic was delighted by this expression of fan support and announced that he intended to play in the game.

Fans of basketball and of Magic Johnson who were looking forward to seeing that game, were not dissapointed. Magic lead the Western Conference team to an amazing 153-113 victory. With twenty-five points, nine assists and five rebounds, Magic put in an impressive performance. When Magic was awarded the All-Star game's Most Valuable Player, the crowd rose to their feet to give him a standing ovation.

On February 16, 1992 Magic's No. 32 was retired by the Lakers in a special halftime ceremony. But Magic, as a spokesman for AIDS education, was a long way from retirement.

He had big plans to push for more funds for AIDS research and education. He intended to be a hard-working member of the President's Commission on AIDS. He was determined to get the word out to young people about safe sex. He felt he had been called upon by God to do so. Magic explained his sense of mission in the November 18, 1991, issue of *Sports Illustrated*: "In everything I've done, He's directed me. This is just another way. Knowing this, how can I look at the infection as anything other than an opportunity to do something that might even overshadow my playing career? Sure, I was convinced that I would never catch the AIDS virus, but it was going to happen to someone, I'm actually glad it happened to me. I think I can spread the message concerning AIDS better than almost anyone."

CAREER STATISTICS

College

Season	Team	GP	FGA	FG%	REB	PTS	AVG
1977-78	Michigan State	30	382	.458	237	511	17.(
1978-79	Michigan State	32	370	.468	234	548	17.
TOTAL		62	752	.462	471	1059	17.

N.B.A. Regualar Season

Season	GP	FGA	FG%	REB	AST	STL	BLK	PTS	AV
1979-80	77	949	.530	596	563	187	41	1,387	18
1980-81	37	587	.532	320	317	127	27	798	21
1981-82	78	1,036	.537	751	743	208	34	1,447	18
1982-83	79	933	.548	383	829	176	47	1,326	16
1983-84	67	780	.565	491	675	150	49	1,178	17
1984-85	77	899	.561	476	968	113	25	1,406	18
1985-86	72	918	.526	426	907	113	16	1,354	18
1986-87	80	1,308	.522	504	977	138	36	1,909	23
1987-88	72	996	.492	449	858	114	13	1,408	19
1988-89	77	1,137	.509	607	988	138	22	1,730	22
1989-90	79	1,138	.480	522	907	132	34	1,765	22
1990-91	79	976	.477	551	989	102	17	1,531	19
Total	874	11,657	.523	6,076	9,721	1,698	361	17,239	19

N.B.A. Playoffs

	GP	FGA	FG%	REB	AST	STL	PTS	AVG
Career	186	2,513	.508	1,431	2,320	358	3,640	19.6

Index

A

Abdul-Jabbar, Kareem, 28, 30, 32-35, 37, 39-40, 44, 48, 50-53, 59-60, 62, 63, 70, 74

Aguirre, Mark, 46, 55

AIDS (acquired immune deficiency syndrome), 68, 71, 72, 74, 75, 77

Australian Olympic team, 75

AZT, 68, 74

B

Bird, Larry, 24, 26, *27*, 28, 32, 35, 43-44, 48, 51, 53, 58, 70

Boston Celtics, 7, 28, 32, 39, 43-44, 48, 50-51, 53, 56-60

Brother Rice High School, 16

Bush, President George, 74

Buss, Jerry, 39-40

C

Chastine, Reggie, 11, *12*, 14, 16

Chones, Jim, 30, 33-34

Cooper, Michael, 33, 63-64

Cunningham, Billy, 35

D

Dallas Mavericks, 46, 52-53, 55

ddI, 68

Denver Nuggets, 50

DePaul University, 23-24

Detroit Catholic Central High School, 13-14

Detroit Northeastern High School, 13

Detroit Pistons, 28, 46, 56-57

Donnelly, Terry, 26

Dwight Rich Junior High School, 10

E

Everett High School, 10, 13, 16

F

Fox, George, 10, 13, 16

G

Golden State Warriors, *42*, 56

H

Heathcote, Jud, 17, 22, 24

Hall, Arsenio, 70

HIV (human immunodeficiency virus), 68, 69, 70, 72, 74

Houston Rockets, 39, 53, 55

I

Indiana State University, 23-24, 26

J

Johnson, Christine, 9, 22, 26, 28, 37, 47

Johnson, Cookie, 66, 69, 74

Johnson, Earvin, Sr., 9, 17, 22, 26, 28
Johnson, Evelyn, 13
Johnson, Larry, 9

K

Kansas City Kings, 38
Kelly, Cookie, 47, 51, 53
Kelser, Gregory, 19-20, 22-23, 26, 28

L

Lamar College, 22
Los Angeles Lakers, 26, 28-30, 32-35, 38, 40-41, 43-44, 48, 50-51, 55-62
Louisiana State University Tigers, 22

M

McAdoo, Bob, 41, 44, 50
McHale, Kevin, 48, 59
McKinney, Jack, 30, 32
Main Street School, 9
Mellman, Dr. Michael, 68, 69, 72
Michigan State University, 16-17, 19-20, 22-24, 16, 37, 53

N

National Basketball Association (NBA), 26, 28-29, 32, 35, 39, 41, 50-51, 53, 56-57, 62
National Commission on AIDS, 74, 77
National Collegiate Athletic Association (NCAA), 20, 22-24
New Jersey Nets, 39

Nixon, Norm, 30, 33, 41, 43, 46
Notre Dame University, 23

O

Olympics, 67, 75

P

Paris, France, 67
Parish, Robert, 44
Phelps, Digger, 23
Philadelphia 76ers, 32-35, 41
Phoenix Suns, 32, 41, 43

R

Riley, Pat, 40-41, 63, 64, 70

S

safe sex, 72
San Diego Clippers, 30
Seattle Supersonics, 32, 52, 56
Sexton High School, 10, 13
Stabley, Fred, Jr., 11

T

Thomas, Isiah, 46-47, 53, 56, 70

U

United Negro College Fund, 53
University of Michigan, 16-17
University of Pennsylvania Quakers, 23
University of Utah, 23-24
Utah Jazz, 26, 40

V

Vincent, Jay, 9, 17, 19, 22-23

W

Western Kentucky University, 20
Westhead, Paul, 32-34, 37, 40
Worthy, James, 41, 44, 50, 55, 60